AF446960

GOING FOR A RIDE SOMEWHERE

Cracker crumbs!
White people particulars, you know
just ordinary guys
leasing their guns
to a next door neighbor
of similar persuasion
without reason to suspect or feel
trepidation
when the fair produce fires
its flash of the sun

like a door slamming shut
or like quiet rubber tires.

SMOKE AND GHOSTS

Flower and root of my heart1!
Wine and nectar of my veins!

...as much as God and poems
you are
the reason that I live.

What meaning do they have
if you are gone
before I die?

...cigarettes again!
all of the ash of silly song!
all of the prayers to a silly lie!

THE GOLDEN CHILD WITHIN

How will I ever forgive
that sore selfish lazy part of myself
now old and wrinkled
and sulking with tears
in the corner of a house
belonging to an old woman
who laughs like wine
and gives me shelter.

THE DESAPAIR WITHIN

Yawns in the dark room
infuse the lungs with stale air
in shivering mid autumn
whose cold black stare
leans out toward dusty clouds beyond
that window where the cars belong
on streets full of sadness
and a sigh
for such an age's lullaby!

SUBLIMINAL

The furry rabbit had to piss.
In petaled nest
or purple bliss
such water stokes
an ancient urge
more fundamental than his sex.

And in a second blood was spilled!
The falcon dropped. The day was killed.

A sunny day! Sunlight kissed
a night
which came to rot that way.

SECRETS OF THE SWAMP

Hell has descended on us!
He is a fat pink vulgar slob
full of arrogance
and self pity

...the city
blooms a black flower
out toward its rural expanse.

Pale dullards much like hell
are the ruin of us all!
The rock uncovered bares its ants.
A wet and tepid winter
come of Fall.

FIRST SIGNS OF MORNING

I would hope that the darkness subsides slowly
...it shields me.
And the light which comes
in Winter daylight
bears a tepid ugliness

...not the trees shorn of leaves
which celebrate such a brittle hour
with shards and shadow
through their branches

but   a waft of exhaust
when the days thin traffic begins
with the poison and soot
or this age
and its sins.

THE LOVE BOND

See we are ancient already! We are marble
carved and sealed to fortressed stone
inseparable the way we aged together
and glistening in our polish
like one of your starry paintings.

Or an old rustic house
grown out as one toward the woodland.
We live in the same skin
shelter under each other's locks.

I look out the window of your brilliant eyes
and see and give utterance for the world
eternally brand new!

IN EVERY REAL APOCALYPSE

Headachy brain
like windy pain
in the scorching storms
of summer

while the world and all of its politics
turns sick surreal and hot
in every real apocalypse
and every one that's not.

FAT MAN IN A SUMMER WINDOW

Morning, stormy overcast
bled out to a bright day

....passions died down
to despair.

Sunlight despises me!
I am badly chiseled clay

drying and drowning
in air!

HUNCHES

I guess at everything,
at every notion that I uncover
...my faith is in mysteries
....God and the world
....my lover and our families
and mysterious friends
I have come upon like jewels

....the cat in our house
lives a hidden poetry
...my lover's paintings
are deeper than sex.

If there is pain or dissatisfaction in this
it is the continual nature of human passion
unraveling
and struggling

with mere mortal issues
till beauty and peace
transcend them.

LOOKING BEYOND THE FLOOD

Jesus is still my God, is still my still life prayer
nailed to a ceiling of stars
and crowned with terrible pain
in the middle of sweltering summer
after a steamy rain.

THE SILK OF THE POET'S ANGUISH

Here in the dark I tremble
from that sheer fatigue
of the day

...terrible darkness
bleak with rest
curling the speech of lost words,
lifting the weight of God

...heavy heavy vengeful truths
leaning into night
in the dim computer light!

MINIMALIST TECHNOLOGIES

There is no shadow of time here
on this winter sundial.
Garden under overcast skies
beyond the window
and within, only the dim light of the computer screen.
A program for my eggshell words
on such a frigid day.

WHAT MAKES ME PRAY TO JESUS

Rachel!
Nest of me…comfort in night
firm yet feather soft!
House of mine! yet hidden in the trees
near the circle where the cars all pass
so that this warm place is so much like you

though in the trailer cold some day I'll weep
among the stars and grasses fast asleep.

NIGHTS OF THE PAGAN EMPEROR

Frightened pissy nerves
For such an ancient heap.
Outside the junk car swerves
…inside the night runs deep.

I borrow sex from beauty
made of love
and fall asleep to the cold cold cave
of dreams
that icy cove
that place where frozen waters
drip and seep
their slowly dripping prayers
to death
and Jove.

EVERY MORNING BLOOMS WITH FROST THIS TIME OF YEAR

Every morning blooms with frost this time of year
…icing of the winter cake!
…tears which freeze so sweet
And form the sour-sweet bread we bake.
A solitude of the child, this ancient happy tear.
In danger would the winters grow too warm
…in fire and death would our worst spirits storm

In a maculate return such decadent jungles burn
And form
A winter worse than ice,
A hunger destitute and torn
That such planets might succumb to fire
Never to fall asleep and dreaming form
Renewal of our warm spring season's norm/

2020

Death by a bloody asthma
in years smoked by racism
inhaled in the innards
with a final infection
ready for the respirator
and waiting for election.

GOING FOR A RIDE SOMEWHERE

Cracker crumbs!
White people particulars, you know
just ordinary guys
leasing their guns
to a next door neighbor
of similar persuasion
without reason to suspect or feel
trepidation
when the fair produce fires
its flash of the sun

like a door slamming shut
or like quiet rubber tires.

title pp MY PRYER IS A BLUE PASSAGE

LOW BURN

Fire in the corner and
Cars on the street
Light for a moment your
furrowed brow
The days brighten up much slower now
Through the frosted grill
Now,
With calm of doubt
Set to me eyes
The ashen faith
The hollow glow
Of a love that still burns
Cigarettes at hushed dawn
With the shadow of gray embracing skies
As soft as soft impending snow
On the burrough where our apartment lies

Close your eyes
And blush
Sleep at my feet
And now far away where
Planes take off
And the reaper reaps
A low Moan

Those months are lean
And tender to eat
These months would be salt
To keep our meat
From other days
That the sweeper sweeps
and
As I have a love
For someone to keep
It should be the fire
Next to you
Anyway

WHAT THE LEAVES SEEM TO DO

Autun approaches eternally
My allegiance is to cooler days
The sunlight on misty cells
And on bent leaves

I will stand withered
Beard and sweater
Iberian: dead with the summer holocaust
A catholic crease in my eyes:
Crossed, full of their sorry luck
and good wishes
Dreading the day
Among Carolina evenings
When my bones are too wet and warm
To hold and form against dusk

And the earth circles
Against both my love and restraint
I fold my heart in a pocket of sorts
And breathe the wind in
And dance
Or pretend
To dance

SONG OF THE STRAW MAN

The grasses dry handsomely
and die at an appropriate hour
even with the first frost
too early to be fair.
They are good friends
quite readily.

With my mind
and its febrile eye,
I was neither so good,
nor so fortunate
as to die.

And the wax of winter
flooded all the heartland away,
And I was left,
with land bereft,
with good things gone to hay.

THE MIND CELL

Such days do not speak,
they are torn
and nervous, filled
with footsteps
and neurotic sighs.

We are always jailed
over small things,
webbed in
by our weakness,

and we wait
the long hours
for a friend
who never comes.

DAYS THAT LEAD TO NIGHT

Weak blue sky
and misery
of waking
half endured
and half spit-out
of the mind
like grounds
at the bottom
of the drip-grind.

I take my mornings
slow and hard.

the are:
as much aggrieved
as it is assured,
steps then
out of Wednesday
and of June,
and takes a sickly stroll
searching for a meaning
and a moon.

OLD FRIENDS IN AMERICA

I saw his blank look burden
On the door mat
He may have wanted to shuffle past me
And complain about the neighbors dry grass
Or the dent in his two-year-old Buick

"We're both still unattached"
I murmur that
We eat stale tomato sandwiches
He wears a faded business suit
And half wishes he could write
Instead of teach
"Its a hard game" I assure him
Out the door for three more years

One of us belongs
In a bar in Madrid
The other should lie down
In a simple pine box

PAX AMERICANA

Before a dust light
spreads over the land,
I have a desperate need
to hide this secret in the creepers
amid the smell of a land too ripe
with itself, my sour green disposition.

And the heartland will fade someday
the rapture of money and its love
dip down to something ordinary
underneath the stars.

I will be somewhat old
and a full yellow stalk,
and harvest time and the simple dream
of farmers will mean just what they say
it means.

A SAILOR'S GRAVE

The trials of torn days,
the loneliness: a nervous vigor,
crushed, knowing that no man
is that bright apple
that he longs to be
in the eyes of his creator.

For a bond to God
only the sea shares our remorse,
and at that, at times
the white foam curls destructively;
the noise of desolation
is our calling; the brain dissolves
to thunder, to a ghost
as pure as clouds.

And yet
who would ever
set a course to darkly?

In the mind's eye we travel,
spend each and every other moment
burying the truth.

LOVE POEM FROM RUSSIA

When the sunflowers blossom
they are like your art, breathless
and wavy. The winter snows
are a gospel of pure white
that reminds me of the paleness
of our rapture.

Please send something back
to me; not a gift or trinket
for Customs to balk at,
but a pure stillness like
the light in your smile, a few
words like pearls, a lock of hair
smelling of jasmine.

In winter I wait through hours
of blanched darkness; in summer
the fields erupt without you.

EVOLVING TRUTHS IN NEW YORK CITY

Once
For two days
He lived in a fudge
Colored flat in the Village

A modern American thinker
The descendant equally
Of pioneers and primeval slime
Which now coat the old hotel carpet
--Random caprice of wind
And electrons stirring the nearby
Eternal Hudson

Along those strong
Individual banks
He wakes some days
Sniffs at the sea
And heads for a dock shed
For raw eggs in some stiff
Jack Daniel's
Or at very least
a second rate whiskey
Ah will

And the liquid nature of things
will tell, talk of gut pains
and vomit on vacant pavements
Just behind that grand near to dawn
Seclusion...

Some small sectioned concrete
Divides such lives
His wife still loves
Proud and studious men
But now
He has never been one of them.

SOUTHERN COMFORT

My pallet breathes tincture of burgundy
I could drown in it
Like what changes the puddles red to green
For this is the South
Where factories grow from green hills
Where gulls fly inland
From rubber and oil inhale
the marigold

Not just wine this thing
My thing
But wine of the heart
Makes the rude smooth
Now one crack to cut my tires
Maple fires red orange
Bring the Sun to earth sometimes
Why I saw roses bloom on January
one reddish winter
I remember it I ate pepper with Sylvia
Out on the veranda

Night is coming
The cars have bred
With oil shafts and rude openings
I suppose
At any rate more of them
In wild herds
With headlights glued to towns
And chasing off malingerers with words
Profane demands no hint of supplication

This night is black as good farm soil
It must lie if fallow stupor
Lest it spoil
The origins of evenings
Lie with Sylvia, my wife
now dead and dying even more
Each time I realize I reach the final
Element: the empty drive the pitched house
The cellar door

MY PRAYER IS A BLUE PASSAGE

My prayer is a blue passage.
It is the sea, volatile
and passive. It is the thousand
islands, and their continents
that disappear from it like foam
into the salt-free vegetation
of jungle and canal, into the arid
deserts, their cacti dust and scrawled
invectives, into the frozen dual extremes
made that much more of the fact of water
and of human thirst.

My prayer is not
of the vastness of space
but of that space reflected
star for star by Heaven's pure sheen:
either one in the human heart
and on this single globe
which God entrusted
to his keepers; be they constant
brave and open
in their journeying.

MURMURS OF SUNDAY

True sunlight on the rose
and summer on wisteria. Blood
and blue flower flowing
with casual breezes. At eleven
we hear the bells of St. Andrews
calling to a flock of Episcopalian
martyrs: those who have withstood
the ravish of pronouncements
from TV evangelists and from
a faithless age.

Heaven has become the dominion
of mars and Martians. The earth
is bound up in a belief in anything.
But those who died for love
whisper leafy chronicles, and tired men
surround the church muting their cigars,
pray secretly for hope's return
entering the relics of an ash-gray chapel.

HEAVEN'S TEMPTERS

I surely remember
that I was the Moon
with iced light smile
frozen spite on a river
of bile, gazing like God
on seasons, and men, all
shine and no care in white
forests when

Some autumn hearts fed me
with havens song, to blue me,
to tan me, to mellow my wrong

Then I was a bird
with a shiver and song
and sat with this little fellows
humming their tune, till they wandered
home to feast on a bird, and I surely
remembered why I was the Moon.

ST. PETER AT THE FINAL HOUR

I, ready to shut me eyes
to dawn; I an illiterate
fishermen, insufferably slow
in thought. The Sun
whose patched contours
illuminate Etruscan ruins,
defrost a winter morning,

is over a hill
and in the sky
before I even dream
once more
the skull
that sends me shivering:
Golgatha
and the death of God,
the high cross
and the lonely place
which celebrants
inherit.

My master
called me "rock"
and I sit
upon his petrified throne
stiff with the fear
of swords and ruin
aching for a place
to sleep, as soft
as the shores
of Galilee.

EL SERPIENTE

I know
the vast lay of the land,
the palms and dust here,
know them with my tendrils,
my mouth.

Beauty screams at me.
She is horribly poor,
a kerchief for bandana,
her clothing, wet
with river silt.

I prey on her
in mischief
want her
to rebel

against the Bishops,
the oligarchs, the blue
sky which engulfs her hair.

But she is somehow faithful
to her small days
and her misery.

EL NEGOCIO DE DIOS

Dull sunken eyes
and coins for a psalm

In my mind's eye
I see them
pressing the palm
over wormy water,
or oily indulgences
the fat archbishop
and his brethren
lords of the born
and lords of the dead,
who keep the wine
and shave the bread.

CANTO DOMINICANO

In the dark
the wild streets sound
their sadness. Only now,
the revelry of hurt souls
who refuse to die.

In our suffering
we have soft island nights;
the sea-breeze suffocates
and we embrace our lovers
like a memory of God.

And God will come to us
one rainy morning,
one horrible preponderance
of sweat and heat and storm

bearing gifts of the season

till then our sweet thoughts
bloom at night:
scent of orchid
or papaya
waiting
aching
to be born.

SWAMP GUILE

No one knows
that in such a humid transparency
my illness found a strange kind of flowering
among ferns and hibiscus. Mermaid figures
arrived at the dank edge of my trailer
full breasted and innocently mocking
morning twilight. When I stared hard
the log appeared indifferently
the scaly fungi at the fish-tail.

Afternoons,
my therapist took me out
to throw a line and catch some brim
at the river's edge. He was a good
man and knew
how to weed the world with worms.

I learned to gut the catch,
scale them, flower and fry them
in a greased skillet.

This is the aching sacrifice
to eat the cousin to all perfect lovers,
grinning spitting bones, alive
in the round ghoulish moonlight
of Friday and of summer.

I bleed
against the parapets
of city doorways now,
know again, quite sanely,
that no human form
is sacred, from
the wet womb of things.

A RUN THROUGH WHATS LEFT OF A TARHEEL LIFE

A fog has settled on the farm
The briar lewaves have touched me
with their thorns
As clouds hang on tobacco barns
and old tired dreams reborn
Though I may see that weathered sun
orange in morning
the way water colors run

Down the shallow of the stream I run
Down the breast of August days
and up the far bank of the road
The crow downs with a scream
toward far banks and ground
as sweet as stoic bitter
a teasing myth
a thorny sound
in swirls of separating mist
and early autumn haze

I do not love these southern summers
more or less
than crucifixions full of thorns and nails
rotting rust and tortured flesh

But bodies need their bials of faith and rain
rustic and blood red in welded weather vanes
as old souls need to weep and grieve
above the seed of better days
leave their burn through Augsus agony
resting in a shallow grave to pray
and prove some tired test.

www.ingramcontent.com/pod-product-compliance
Lightning Source LLC
Chambersburg PA
CBHW081937120726
47997CB00010B/3170